Unearthing

Unearthing
The History of Argyle
©2025 Louise Mitchell

Published by Hobo Jungle Press
St. Vincent & the Grenadines, W.I.
Sharon, Connecticut, USA

ISBN #979-8-9897406-8-0

First edition
January 2025

All rights reserved. No part of this publication may be reproduced, distributed, or transmitted in any form or by any means, including photocopying, recording, or other electronic or mechanical methods, without the prior written permission of the publisher, except in the case of brief quotations embodied in critical reviews and certain other noncommercial uses permitted by copyright law.

The photograph on the cover shows the original petroglyph site at Argyle with the foliage that existed prior to the removal project. Some hand-drawn depictions of the petroglyphs found at Yambou I site and the neighbouring Yambou VIII site have been superimposed on the photo. The statue depicts the Christian image of the Virgin Mary placed within a replica apse creating a shrine. This was the brainchild of Benedictine Missionary Charles Verbeke who served in St. Vincent in the 1940s. He claimed this sacred Amerindian site reminded him of Lourdes in France. It too, like Lourdes, became a place of pilgrimage for Catholics. Before the petroglyph rocks were extracted the statue of the Virgin was removed and secured by the Catholic Church.

Throughout history there is evidence of one religion building monuments on top of the holy places of other religions in an effort to demonstrate the superiority of their belief system. This may be one such incident. Of course, it is also possible that the Catholics simply felt this site to be one with a particularly special energy, as did the Amerindians, and wanted to harness that energy as a place of worship.

Cover design by Nadia Huggins
Cover Photo: Holly Bynoe
Drawings of Petroglyphs by Hayssam Moubayed

Unearthing the History of Argyle

Written and edited by
Louise Mitchell

with additional contributions by
Kathy Martin, Deirdre Millington-Myers,
Nicola Redway, and Dr. Adrian Fraser

UNEARTHING THE HISTORY OF ARGYLE

Introduction

In 2008, St. Vincent and the Grenadines was ready to move ahead with construction of an international airport at Argyle. There was one thing in the way, however: a mountain of basalt rock near the mouth of the Yambou River on which existed a cluster of some of the most amazing petroglyphs ever found on St. Vincent, known as Yambou I.

As custodian of all things heritage, the St. Vincent and the Grenadines National Trust was charged with the difficult task of determining the fate of the petroglyphs. One thing was certain: they could not remain where they were, as this mountain of rock presented a protrusion that was too near the proposed runway to remain in place.

In the field of archeology, it is considered sacrilege to move an object from its original location. Before taking such drastic action, archaeologists consider the legal and ethical aspects of moving the objects, as well as their significance and the potential impact on understanding the site and its history. Given that the alternatives were either to move the petroglyphs or lose them, the National Trust decided that moving them was the lesser of two evils.

Before any action was taken, the petroglyph site was visited by Geologist/Volcanologist Professor Ritchie Robertson of the University of the West Indies' Seismic Research Center. Professor Robertson warned that in moving the petroglyphs, there was a chance they could splinter into pieces, resulting in the loss of the 2000-year-old images on them. While the National Trust laboured over a solution, they pushed ahead with excavations at Argyle, as it was certain that near the petroglyphs was a rich heritage site. Amazing discoveries were made and a trove of artifacts was uncovered, many of which are now on display at the Carnegie Building in Kingstown.

At the forefront of these discoveries was the Argyle Heritage Action Plan, designed by Kathy Martin, the former chair of the National Trust. The plan included excavations that unearthed the first ever Cayo village. Also on the site of the runway were the ruins of the Argyle Sugar Mill. The Trust invited students from the USA to draw the ruins the way they were; subsequently, all the relics from the Estate that were mobile enough to be moved were transported to a site at Escape (about a half mile away), where the Government had allocated lands for the National Trust to create an outdoor museum about the cultural history of Argyle, from petroglyphs to sugar plantations to East Indian migration. The Escape site (which also contained ruins) was proposed for the relocation of the petroglyphs. During the construction of the airport — and despite calls from the Trust to leave the Escape Sugar Mill ruins intact — a road was cut through the site to build a new inland highway to remove traffic from the coastal road. In the process of building the road, about a third of the Mill was struck down, lost for all time.

Subsequent to the above actions, the Trust reached far and wide to find experts who would be able to safely remove and relocate the petroglyphs. Initially, Kayandel Archaeological Services, an Australian group, came up with some ideas, but the cost was prohibitive (half a million dollars). Then, as chair of the Trust — having spent a year in Egypt — I revived an old Egyptian contact to see if Egypt's archaeologists could help, given their huge expertise in the preservation of artifacts. After all, they moved Abu Simbel, one of the greatest challenges of archaeological engineering history. Surely, they could move Yambou I. Alas, the Arab Spring beginning in 2010 aborted plans the Egyptians had to use a diamond saw to excise the petroglyphs rocks.

Frustration was growing within the Government; the delay in finding a solution meant major delays in construction of the airport. Then one day, an archaeologist from Argentina showed up in the office of the SVG National Trust, apparently due to a request from someone in foreign affairs that SVG needed support in the preservation of its archaeological past. Upon meeting Dr. Monica Beron, I indicated to her that we needed help with the moving of the petroglyphs; before long, Dr. Beron, Trust Manager Lavern Bentick Phillips, Morrison Baisden, and I were on a site visit to Argyle. The rest is history.

Having successfully extricated the rock faces with the images from Argyle (documented in a movie entitled *Messages in the Rock*), the next step The National Trust took was to develop a park where the petroglyphs would be showcased to the world, together with the relics of the Argyle Sugar Mill and the Escape Sugar Mill. The Trust was allocated two acres of land at Escape, close to the original site of the petroglyphs, and charged with presenting the rich cultural history of Argyle. To honour the work of Kathy Martin, who devised the Argyle Heritage Action Plan, and her husband Christian "Cims" Martin, CMG, who founded the Heritage Fund to support the work of the Trust, it was agreed that the site be named the Martins Petroglyph Park. While the petroglyphs are certainly the highlight of the park, it is also intended to showcase the entire history of Argyle from indigenous times through to slavery and the days of sugar plantations, stretching into the period of indentureship, when a strong Indian culture took root in Argyle.

This little book sets about telling the story of Argyle, which will become the basis for signs to be erected on the site of the Petroglyph Park. I was supported in the effort of researching and writing about the history of Argyle and the petroglyphs by Kathy Martin, Deirdre Millington-Myers, Dr. Adrian Fraser, and Nicola Redway. The history retold herein recalls the settlement of St. Vincent and the Grenadines starting with the arrival of the first Amerindians in dugout canoes, through to colonial times and the indentureship period, when East Indian migration added to Argyle's cultural pot. The history of Argyle is indicative of the history of St. Vincent and the Grenadines as a whole: diverse and resilient.

The special energy one feels in the presence of the petroglyphs is in knowing that some 2000 years ago, someone carved this rock with a message that was intended to pass from generation to generation. It is our duty to read these messages and to continue to tell the story of our peoples' journey of resilience and fortitude through the ages.

- Louise Mitchell
December 17th, 2024

PART I

The St. Vincent Petroglyphs

Petroglyphs are rock carvings, images or forms created by incising, picking, carving or abrading the surface of rocks. Tools made from hard minerals such as quartz and jade, and from the volcanic glass obsidian were used to draw the patterns into the rock. Peck marks from the engraver's subsequent work with a stone hammer and chisel are visible on some images.

The Lascaux caves of southwest France contain some of the most renowned rock art in the world, where there are hundreds of paintings, many etched into the ceilings of a network of caves. This art is estimated to be from the Upper Paleolithic period, which took place around 17,000 to 15,000 BCE.

Student Jamie Joachim at the Martins' Petroglyph Park

Similarly, in the United States there can be found native American rock art throughout the country; a famous example is known as Newspaper Rock, found in the Canyonlands National Park of Utah.

The petroglyphs of St. Vincent and the Grenadines embody iconic imagery created by the Amerindian peoples who arrived on the islands in dugout canoes from the Lower Orinoco region of South America.

These stone carvings are set among cliffs, streams and forest glades; they are carefully oriented to capture the light patterns of the sun, shade, stars, and moon. The serenity of these sites suggests that they were sacred and ceremonial with much time devoted to their creation.

Chateaubelair Cup Holes. Photo: Louise Mitchell.

In St. Vincent, there can be found several different types of rock engravings. The first category is drawings/images, of which all remaining ones are found on the mainland of St. Vincent. The petroglyphs at Argyle fall into this first category and are the focus of this booklet. The second category is cupules or cup holes — also known as work stones — utilitarian in nature, used to create and sharpen tools or grind foods, mix potions and pigments. These hemispherical, cup-like hollows like the ones at Sandy Bay are the most common on St. Vincent. They are mainly found next to a body of water, usually the bay side. There are dozens of such work stones found both on the mainland of St. Vincent and in the Grenadines (Spring Bay on Bequia being one site in the Grenadines). The third type of petroglyph is the cupules which appear to be ceremonial in nature, as their designs and frequency are such that they do not appear to have a utilitarian purpose. The Chateaubelair 13 stones, with clusters of cupules, line a magical wooded pathway leading towards the sea near Chateaubelair islet, with vistas of the majestic La Soufriere. It is possible that the cupules were used for ritualistic purposes, maybe even paying homage to the power of the great volcano. Examples of rock art and pottery are the most significant physical evidence that migrating peoples from South America settled on the islands of the Caribbean. Rock art with similar imagery found in the Guianas, Brazil and Venezuela, are also evident on the islands from Trinidad in the south to The Bahamas in the north.

Dating petroglyphs is challenging because they are essentially engravings on stone, made using stone, and therefore do not contain carbon. Radiocarbon dating is a method for determining the age of material that contains organic material.

Some theories, based on stylistic evidence, suggest that the petroglyphs on St. Vincent and the Grenadines may date from the Saladoid period (300 BCE–650 CE) of settlement in the Caribbean.

The pottery art of this period includes very sophisticated white-on-red designs, and many Saladoid pottery sherds were found at Argyle in the area of the petroglyphs.

Other theories suggest that the petroglyphs were created much later, during the Suazoid period (1000 CE–1500 CE). Pottery from other ceramic ages was also found in the same location.

Most of the petroglyphs of St. Vincent and the Grenadines are anthropomorphic (depicting human faces and other human features), similar to those found on the trail from the Orinoco to The Bahamas. Other petroglyphs depict images of a rayed head or a Sun God, which are reminiscent of images found in Africa. Stone tools and sherds of quartz, jade, and volcanic glass obsidian were retrieved at Argyle and Escape during archaeological investigations undertaken during construction of the Argyle International Airport.

The Buccament Cave site is unique on St. Vincent where the imagery on the main panel is not anthropomorphic or zoomorphic (depicting animal features), but rather geometric and abstract script.

The Egyptian archaeological team who worked on the relocation of the Yambou I petroglyphs also paid a singular visit to the Buccament petroglyphs. Their impression was that these petroglyphs may have been done by a different group of people at an earlier period in time. This impression supports the possibility that St. Vincent may have been inhabited by Africans prior to the arrival of the indigenous peoples from South America. The glyphs appear somewhat similar to the Arabic script. Of interest is the fact that the number of persons of African descent reported to have been on St. Vincent around the time of European contact is exceptionally high.

Buccament Bay Cave Petroglyphs. Photo: Holly Bynoe.

A Plan to Save the Petroglyphs

The Yambou I Petroglyphs, located near the mouth of the Yambou River, were likely to be destroyed due to the alignment of the proposed runway for the new Argyle International Airport. Recognising the imminent loss, the SVG National Trust, under the chairmanship of Mrs. Kathy Martin, in 2008 created the Heritage Action Plan for the Argyle International Airport Site, in order to *"… mitigate the scale of the overall impact of the project on the cultural heritage and to avoid the ultimate loss of cultural assets and important information on the history of St. Vincent."*

The SVG National Trust engaged teams of archaeological experts to provide the road map for the safe removal of the petroglyphs and related artefacts.

Prior to the commencement of the exercise to dislodge and remove the panels of rock, volcanologist at the UWI Seismic Research Unit, Dr. Richie Robertson, visited the site and cautioned that it was possible that the rock may split while being removed from the surrounding parent rock.

The Trust engaged Dr. Eric Pélissier, an experienced museum modeller from Guadeloupe, to create two moulds of the petroglyphs in situ, so that the original images could be preserved for all time in the event that the actual petroglyphs were damaged during the move. One of these moulds is on display at the National Trust Headquarters at the Carnegie Building in Kingstown.

The Archaeological teams included:

- The team from the Egyptian Ministry of Culture. In 2011, they developed a plan to remove the entire cliff face that contained the engraved panels and to reconstruct it in a similar setting and orientation achievable at the proposed Escape Park. The team, headed by Dr. Abu al Dardaa, also included Khalad Mostafa, Mostafa Elattar and Ashraf Nageh.

- The Kayandel Archaeological Services. In 2012, this specialist archaeological and cultural heritage company from New South Wales, Australia, executed the first-ever survey of the rock face using 3D laser technology. They produced fine digital imaging of the individual engravings and identified several new engravings. The team included Dr. Lance Syme, Ben Gunn and Cliff Ogelby.

- The Argentinian team, led by archaeologist Dr. Monica Beron, with geologist Dr. Horacio Villalba, Dario Guayanes, and Juan Pablo was the team that successfully extracted the petroglyphs from the Yambou I site, building on the work of previous teams. Vincentian mechanic Lawson Byam assisted them and supervised the extraction of Panel A and Yambou VIII after their return to Argentina.

The actual execution of the project to extract the Yambou I petroglyphs was carried out by the Argentinian team in 2014, together with the National Trust under the chairmanship of Louise Mitchell, working in conjunction with the International Airport Development Company. The Yambou VIII panel was extracted in 2015.

Removing the Petroglyphs

1. A series of holes were drilled into the rock face, in which expansive cement was poured. The resulting chemical reaction caused the rock to quietly split along the line of the holes.

2. Larger rocks were removed using strategically placed dynamite with controlled non-destructive explosions.

3. Where there was a natural crack in the rocks, a series of holes were drilled along the cracks into which wedges were driven to create the separation. This method was used to remove smaller rocks from the cliff face.

4. A backhoe was used to remove the adjacent rocks and to provide support to the panels of engraved stones as they were dislodged. Once dislodged, the stones were wrapped in a protective layer of canvas and secured with a heavy chain. The backhoe lifted the wrapped stones to safety. Certain larger panels were lifted by a crane.

A backhoe supports a rock panel which has already been dislodged. Canvas is wrapped around the panel, before its removal using a pulley and crane. (Argentinian team leader Dr. Monica Beron in foreground, Lawson Byam standing in white hard hat).

The Yambou Petroglyphs

*Original Yambou I site before clearing and identification
Photos: Holly Bynoe and Kathy Martin.*

Yambou I site showing identification of individual panels to be excavated and relocated.

YAMBOU I: Panel A – Images 1 and 2

These images of two rayed heads held a high position on the original rock face, approximately seven metres above ground level, suggesting that they were venerated individuals in the sky and spirit realm of the three-part cosmos: underworld, earth and human domain, skies.

Rayed heads are rare motifs in the Antilles, so far found only in St. Vincent and Guadeloupe. They are common in South America, particularly in the Guianas, from where the people who lived in the Cayo Village at Argyle originated.

Image 1 – Depicts a somewhat weathered rayed head, which was clearly originally more complex than that which is now visible, probably similar to Image 2. Concentric eyes and some radials are evident, but details have been lost through exfoliation. Water would have once flowed over the left half of the motif, creating substantive erosion.

Image 2 – Depicts a rayed head resting on a swaddled body, possibly representing the Amerindian funeral practice of binding the mortal remains of the dead. Evidence of this practice was found at the Escape site where Saladoid burials were excavated in 2010.

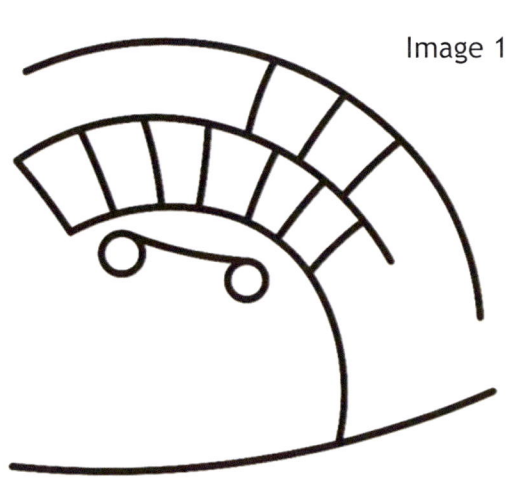

Image 1

Image 2

YAMBOU I: Panel B – Image 7

A singular stylised face imposed on a limbless rectangular body. This figure is distinctive in having almond shaped eyes which are joined by a loop over the forehead.

Image 7

YAMBOU I: Panels D and E

Panels D and E each contained a single image of a face with large eyes and an open mouth. The joined eye-ear motif on panel E is the same as the westernmost one on panel C, only, at 59cm x 64cm, much larger. Like all the other images on the site, they were made by repeat pecking into hard basalt rock (Moh's scale 8). They remained visible despite having endured extreme weathering, suggestive of considerable age. Judging from the fact that only one highly weathered figure has been identified on each of Panels D and E, it is highly likely there were several other images there that could only be visualised under certain weather conditions. It is also possible the surfaces were reused over time. This adds to the wonder of what CAN be seen and imagined when observing the glyphs. For example, on the main Panel C, in addition to the four main figures that are highly visible, in certain light you can sometimes see parts of other figures.

The petroglyphs of Panels D and E are documented in "The Petroglyphs of Yambou 1: A Detailed Recording" — a report to the Kayandel Archaeological Services and the St. Vincent and the Grenadines National Trust by R.G. Gunn and L.C. Douglas (May 2012, page 9) — as images 12 and 13, and classified there as of poor and very poor quality, respectively. Rock 13 has many fracture lines that impact clarity. It is possible these two images are the most recent at Yambou 1, as pecking seems less defined, perhaps a work in progress.

These panels, after having been removed, suffered a further fate of a fire being set right next to them with burning tyres, so much so they became fully unrecognizable and hence are not on display at the Heritage Park

YAMBOU I: Panel C – Images 3, 4, 5, 6

Panel C was the first panel to be removed by the Argentinian team. It contains multiple images, of which four are very clear and are displayed here. The remaining images are vestiges of previous engravings only visible in certain light conditions.

Image 3 is a head-foot figure with an ornate headdress. Head-foot images were first created when Amerindians migrated to the Antilles. They are not present in continental rock art.

Images 4, 5 and 6 are highly stylized faces with open eyes and mouths. Image 6 appears without "ears."

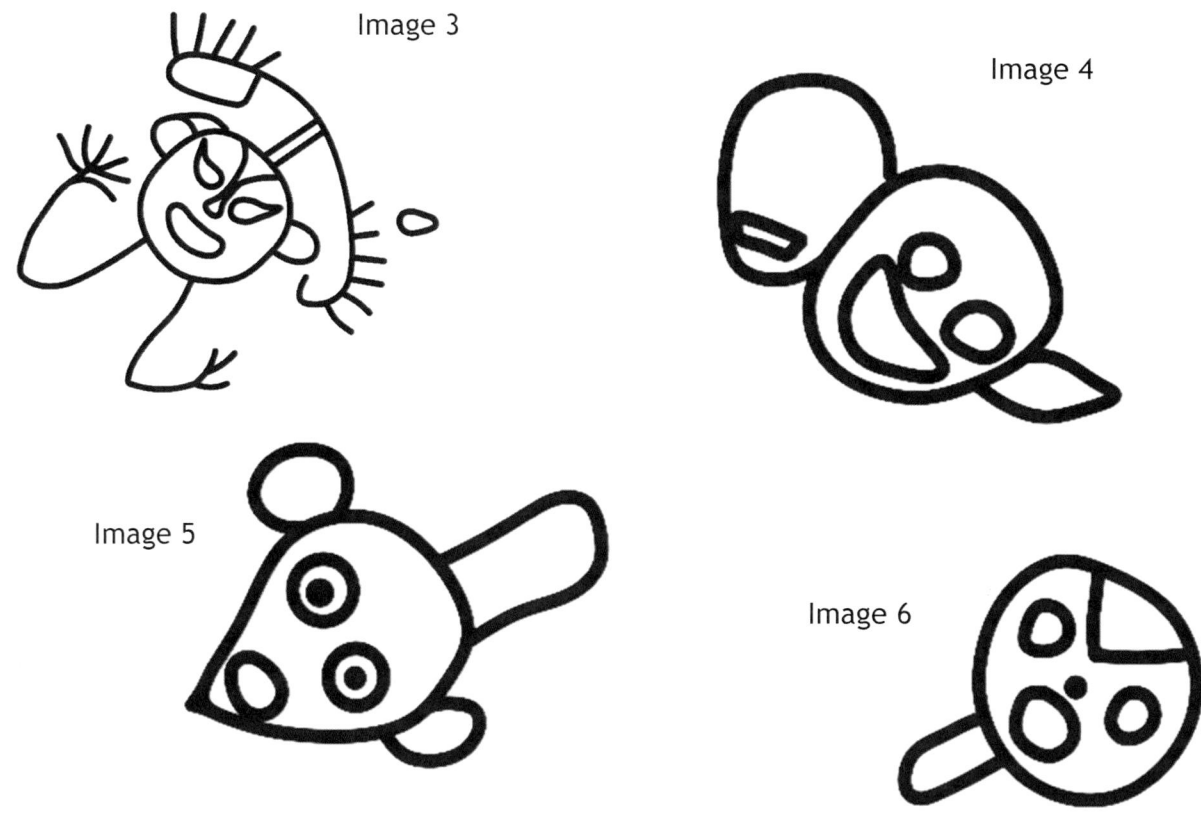

YAMBOU I: Panel F – Image 14

The petroglyph on this stone panel depicts a round, stylised face with pronounced circular and full lips.

This facial form is typical of Caribbean rock art, and many comparable examples are known throughout the region.

Image 14

Image 16

YAMBOU I: Panel H – Image 16

Image 16 is a simple rounded face, identified to the SVG National Trust by primary school student, James Fabian Mitchell, while on a school field trip to Yambou I site.

It was located on the same basalt rock face approximately 20 metres to the east of the cluster of glyphs and at an approximate height of 1.65 metres above ground level.

Petroglyphs in Saint

St. Vincent and the Grenadines has more petroglyphs than any island in the Lesser Antilles except Guadeloupe.

There are 21 known sites of petroglyphs falling into the categories of images and/or scripts, including one that the SVG National Trust has named Yambou VIII – very recently discovered in July 2015, during the construction of the Argyle International Airport. These sites are:

1. Yambou I: Argyle Airport/Catholic shrine area relocated to the Petroglyph Park (multiple images).
2. Yambou II: Mesopotamia Valley (multiple images)
3. Yambou III: Mesopotamia Valley (multiple images)
4. Yambou IV: Mesopotamia Valley (a pattern of cup holes)
5. Yambou V: Mesopotamia Valley (multiple images)
6. Yambou VI: Mesopotamia Valley (multiple images)
7. Yambou VII: Mesopotamia Valley (multiple images)
8. Yambou VIII: Argyle Airport/mouth of Yambou River passing under airport, now relocated to the Escape Petroglyph Park (multiple images)
9. Indian Bay: (single main image)
10. Sharpes Stream: (multiple images)
11. Lowmans Bay: (geometric)

Vincent and the Grenadines

12. Buccament Bay Cave: (multiple script-like images, plus side panels of anthropomorphic images)
13. Layou: (multiple images)
14. Mount Wynne: (geometric with multiple engraved holes)
15. Peter's Hope: (single image)
16. Barrouallie: Ogham Stone (a work stone with slit-like impressions resembling the Celtic Ogham language has since been moved to Walliabou Heritage Park)
17. Barrouallie: Original location Glebe, then Barrouallie Secondary School, has been moved to Walliabou Heritage Park (single image)
18. Petit Bordel: (multiple images)
19. Colonarie: (multiple images, some script-like)
20. Canouan: (single image, now destroyed)
21. Petit St. Vincent Rock: (single image)

In addition to the petroglyphs listed above, there are numerous sites featuring cup holes and work stones, two of the most significant being the Chateaubelair 13 stones and the Sandy Bay work stones.

Sources:

Kirby, I.A. Earle, *Pre-Columbian Monuments in Stone* (St. Vincent Archaeological and Historical Society, 1969; second printing, 1977)

Martin, Kathy, *Set in Stone: The Rock Art of St. Vincent and the Grenadines* (St. Vincent and the Grenadines National Trust, 2011). Available for sale at the National Trust, Carnegie Building, Kingstown.

YAMBOU I: Panel G – Image 15

Image 15 is part of a new discovery made by the National Trust in 2015 during the removal process at the very top of the rock face approximately 10 metres above the existing ground level.

During removal from the site, the rock panel unfortunately broke into two pieces, resulting in damage to the edges.

Tracing of the entire image was therefore tricky; image 15 depicts only the image found on one of the two broken pieces, although traces of engravings can also be seen on the second piece.

The simple, abstract nature of the present design shows stylistic similarities with those found at Sharpes Stream, close to Kingstown: a triangular body with a form of "halo" at the far extremity of the figure.

Image 15

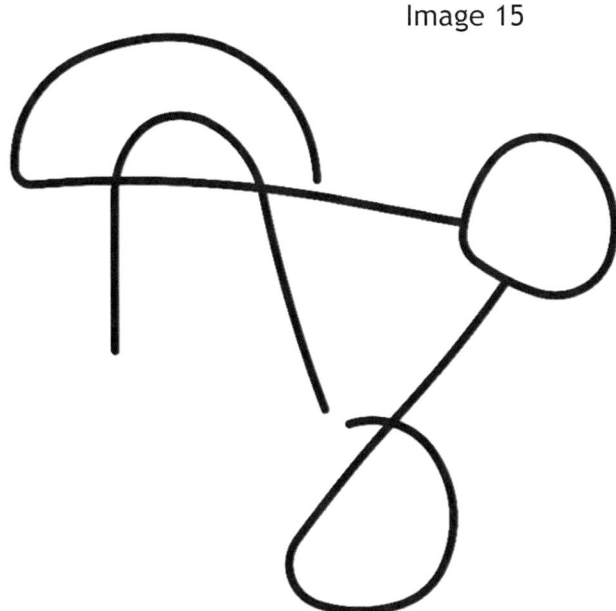

YAMBOU VIII: Images 1, 2, 3, 4

This group of petroglyphs was discovered during the construction of the Argyle International Airport in July 2015, a year after the removal of the other petroglyphs by the Argentinian team — working in conjunction with the National Trust — was completed.

A male construction worker assigned to the realignment of the Yambou River of the Argyle International Airport Project and aware of the rock art at Yambou I, recognised similar images from a previously buried stone. He drew his discovery to the attention of Deirdre Myers, a Trustee of the National Trust, who frequently walked the airport site during construction.

At the time of discovery, the stone was approximately 200 metres northeast of Yambou I in the flood plains of the river. The top of the boulder was approximately one metre below sea level, in contrast to most other known petroglyphs that were discovered on rocks at relatively higher elevation. This suggests the rock was buried beneath centuries-old soil and other debris either in that location, or more likely, after being transported downstream by the rushing waters of the Yambou River during a powerful rainstorm event.

An additional cluster of six petroglyph sites known as Yambou II to VII are all located further upstream of the river, northwest of Yambou I, in the Mesopotamia Valley.

Attempts to remove the Yambou VIII petroglyphs without the supervision of the National Trust resulted in significant damage to the rock and the complete loss of one design along with details of the headdress of the female figure. The photograph shows the lost image located to the left of the female figure.

Close examination revealed at least six images, of which only four survived. The

Trustee Deirdre Millington-Myers measures the new Yambou VIII find.

Image 1

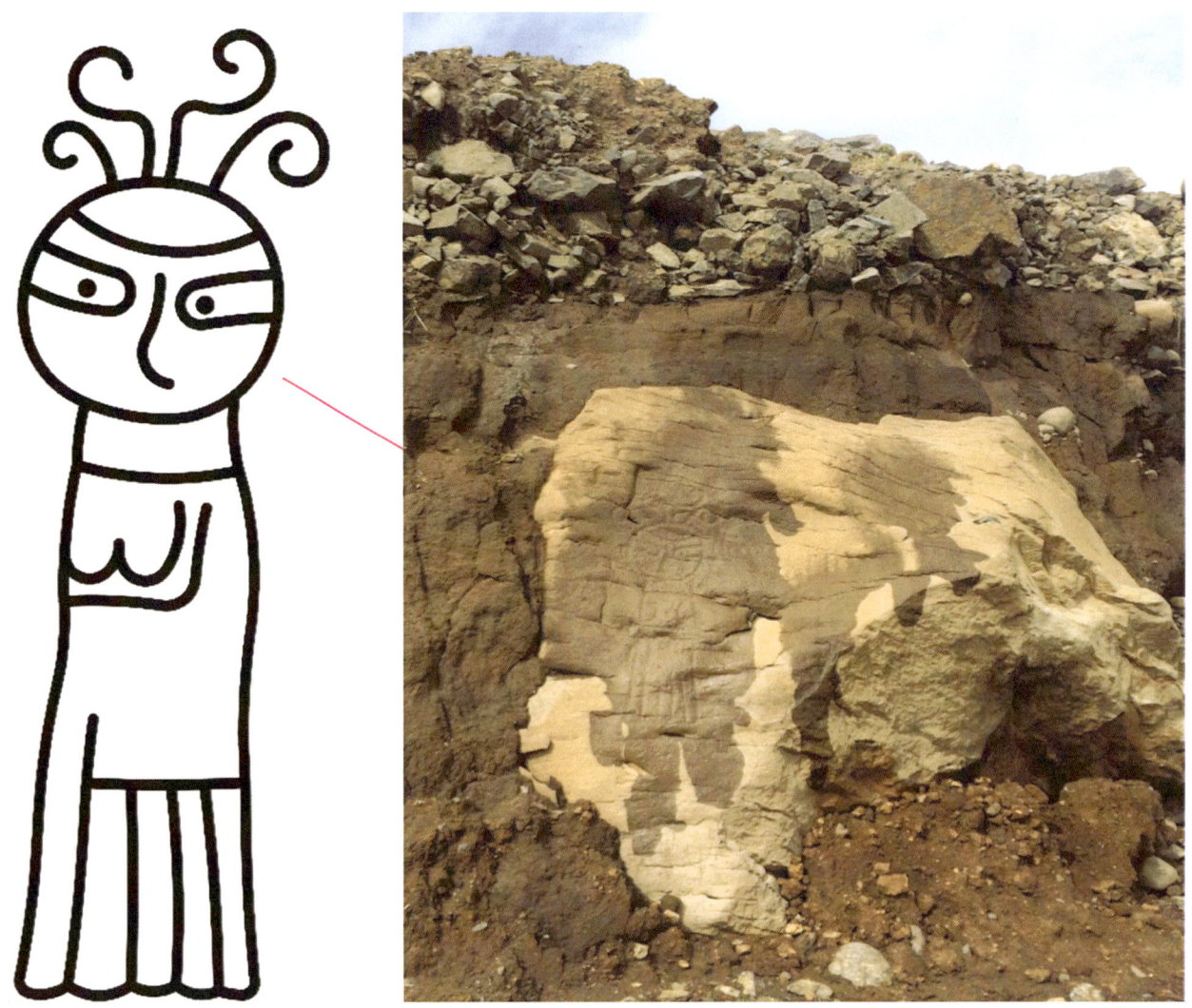

Yambou VIII in its original location, now on display at the Martins Petroglyph Park.

largest and most remarkable of these is the standing female figure complete with elaborate headdress, full 'skirt', and clearly depicted breasts.

This Yambou VIII rock panel with the four remaining designs was ultimately successfully detached from the main rock and moved by Lawson Byam under the supervision of The National Trust.

Image 2

Image 3

Image 4

2012 – Archaeological Excavations at Argyle

by Kathy Martin

(Editor's note: Anticipating that the new airport would occupy the landscape of one of the richest archaeological sites in St. Vincent, under the leadership of Kathy Martin, and in collaboration with the Government, the National Trust undertook a series of archeological digs in the years leading up to the start of construction of the Argyle International Airport. I invited Kathy Martin to share here, in her own words, some of the highlights of those excavations, and what they revealed about our past.)

Long long ago, nearly 2000 years before the present, our ancestors made the area we now call Argyle their home. They were Amerindians from the Orinoco in South America. We know this because they left their Saladoid pots behind. Their dear departed remained too, laid to rest usually curled up peacefully in a prone position under the floors of their houses.

Kathy Martin next to one of the shallow graves unearthed at the Escape site at Escape 2009.

Post holes are evident, showing the footprint of a Kalingo long house, part of an entire Kalinago village discovered at Escape.

The National Trust, in collaboration with the International Airport Development Company, brought teams of archaeologists to gather information as the bulldozers scraped away the top soil. They were joined by volunteers from all over the country, keen to find out about these people.

The professionals knew where to look, as people in the community had reported ancient finds; also, researchers had already dug test pits. In 2008, promising areas of the Northerly Escape site were excavated by Canadians Joe Moravetz of Bison Historical Services Ltd. and Dr. Richard Callaghan of the University of Calgary. During the following three years, a public archaeology programme operated by Margareta De Guzman's Circle CRM Group made interesting finds at the Argyle 2 site, which proved to be one of the largest sites in the Eastern Caribbean.

Meanwhile, an amazing breakthrough was made at the Argyle site by Professor Dr. Corinne Hofman's team from Leiden University in the Netherlands at the mouth of the Yambou River. Amazing because this site, first discovered by Dr Louis Allaire, was occupied by a single group of people in the 17th century. The only pot sherds found on this site were either Cayoid or

This pot was found during Public Archaeology dig, at Argyle 2, in 2012 run by Margarita De Guzman and Jodi with Circle CRM.

European. "The Island Carib Problem" of the archaeological world had been solved. These Kalinago people were, undisputedly, the ones who met the invading Europeans.

Beautiful pots were found, and exquisite beads to die for. Zemis were sometimes left to protect the deceased and help them on their way to the realm of the spirits. Hearths were evident surrounded by the post holes of structures. Evidence of work abounded with stone axes, adzes, imprints of textiles, grinding stones and food middens.

As time went by, successive generations put their creative energies into new endeavours and pottery became cruder. Troumassoid remains show incense burning was important to them. Later Suazoid pots appeared more utilitarian, although they still retained interesting anthropomorphic adornos giving vessels their spirit.

Ceremony was clearly important and evidenced by beautiful symbolic patterning on semiprecious stone items and utensils. And of course, there are sacred spaces where time and skill was invested to create petroglyph monuments. But that is a story in itself.

View of post holes found suggesting Kalinago long house or possible tobacco drying shed.

Argyle Airport site prior to construction. Arrow depicts location of Yambou I petroglyphs.

PART II

The Sugar Industry in St. Vincent

The rich archeological findings have shown that Argyle was a prime settlement site for the Amerindians, and it was no less so for the Imperialists who displaced them. They took advantage of the access to fresh water from the Yambou River and the large areas of arable land, to set up first tobacco and subsequently thriving sugar plantations there. The ruins of the sugar mill at Escape and relics of the industrial machinery of the Argyle Sugar Mill (all on display at the Heritage Park) lead us into the next chapter of this booklet in Vincentian history: British colonialism, sugar, and enslavement. This booklet touches on the short-lived but indelible history of chattel slavery in St. Vincent through the story of the Argyle and Escape Sugar plantations, a microcosm of what would have transpired across the island.

The first European settlements on St. Vincent were established by the French (dating from 1719), mainly on the Leeward side of the island, as evidenced by the coastal towns with French names such as Chateaubelair and Questelles.

The French settlers operated small-scale farm units, planting a variety of crops such as coffee, cocoa, cotton, tobacco, indigo, and ground provisions. The National Trust unearthed evidence of one such small-scale French farm near to the proposed site of the Petroglyph Park in Argyle. Approximately 60 post holes were found, showing the shape of a rectangular structure 36 metres by 5.5 metres, which was thought to indicate a tobacco drying shed. A cobbled road leading from it was also revealed.

When the island was ceded to the British by the French at the Treaty of Paris in 1763, it can be said the plantation economy of St. Vincent truly began. The British set out to establish a path of mono-culture, establishing the island's dependence on a single crop for over 130 years. The first export of sugar was in 1766.

With the establishment of a plantation economy, the struggle for control of land led to two wars between the British and the Caribs: the First Carib War in 1772-1773 and the Second Carib War from 1795 to 1796. The famous 1776 Byres map shows lands north of the Byera River allocated to the

Caribs after the First Carib War as part of a peace settlement negotiated with Carib chiefs, including Paramount Chief Joseph Chatoyer.

In 1797, those Caribs (Garifuna) who survived the brutal Second Carib War were deported (after a devastating exile to the small, desolate island of Balliceaux where half of them perished), to Roatan, an island off the southern coast of Honduras. They then emigrated to mainland Honduras and subsequently to Belize, Guatemala and Nicaragua, where to this day they exist as a thriving culture in exile. Only a small enclave of Garifuna who defied British control remained in the hills of Greiggs, Gordons (now Gordon Yard) and other areas in the interior of St. Vincent.

After the Garifuna were exiled, the British expanded their sugar plantations to the north of the island. With the establishment of the Sugar City of Georgetown, the plantation economy and slavery fully took hold in St. Vincent.

At the peak of sugar production in 1828, it is estimated that there were about 148 estates in St. Vincent producing sugar, molasses and rum. Sugar was also produced on a small scale in Bequia and Mustique. The proliferation of sugar estates required an accompanying rise of enslaved labour. In 1808, a peak of 25,000 enslaved workers was recorded. In 1833, approximately 112 sugar estates were operating in St. Vincent.

The eventual decline of the sugar industry was fostered by owner absenteeism, poor management, the development of alternative sugar from beets, and the high cost of imports following the American War of Independence. The Abolition Act of 1834 (when children under six years of age were freed) came at a time when sugar was already a faltering industry. After the Act was passed, slaves had to work ¾ of the week for their masters under a period of "apprenticeship". This was to allow the plantation owners time to adjust to a new social order. Under the terms of the Abolition Act, if slaves worked beyond ¾ of the working week they would receive low wages. The "apprentices" continued working for their masters until August 1, 1838, which marked the end of apprenticeship and the true end of slavery.

A further injustice was meted out to the former enslaved upon Emancipation In 1838, when about £20 million pounds (£2,778,698,571 in today's currency[1]) was paid in compensation to slave owners throughout the British colonies. This amounted to about £26/slave (£3,612 in today's currency[2]) in St. Vincent.

---

[1] £20,000,000 in 1838 = 2024 | UK Inflation Calculator. Official Inflation Data, Alioth Finance, 15 Jan. 2024, officialdata.org/uk/inflation/1838?amount=20000000.

[2] Ibid

The institution of slavery involved not only offences against human dignity, but the stripping of all African cultural practices and beliefs; even African names were erased and replaced with European ones, as is reflected in the surnames we hear in today's Vincentian society. The former enslaved workers, although now free, received nothing by way of compensation for being enslaved. Slavery also ensured that no education or proper skill-sets were taught to the enslaved, thereby instituting a system of class and privilege that persisted even post-Emancipation.

Many sugar estates failed during the next 100 years and beyond, some ravaged by hurricanes and volcanic eruptions. A few remained well into the 20th century, while some converted their use to arrowroot production.

The last sugar factory in operation on St. Vincent was the Mount Bentinck Sugar Factory at Georgetown, which was finally closed in 1984. The Government privatized the factory and converted it to a rum distillery. Today, the distillery is in private hands but is still in operation, making the famous "Sunset" rum, based on the same traditional production techniques of the sugar estates.

The slave trade between Africa and the British West Indies was abolished by Britain in 1807. This immediately impacted the cost of the production of sugar as the plantation owners had to look after the dependents of enslaved persons until they were of the age to work on the plantations.

Long after abolition, the lives of the freed slaves continued to be restricted by the lack of access to freehold property. Immediately after emancipation, the former enslaved moved away from plantations and started leasing land on the edge of plantations. However it was not until 1899 Resettlement Scheme, when the 1897 West India Commission acquired over 8,500 acres of the 42,000 acres in possession by large landowners, that a measure of land reform was commenced. However, ownership was not enough to restore balance and justice to society as it was not coupled with high wages and most of the land acquired was of poor quality and much of it not suitable for agricultural activity. A further land development scheme followed with the Moyne Commission of 1938-1939.[3] This was followed by the Shepherd Report which recommended agricultural credit for farmers. Land reform would continue into the modern era, and would take centre stage of the Alliance Government of Ebenezer T Joshua and James Mitchell in 1972-74. Both leaders shared a joint vision to improve the lives of agricultural workers, and their land reform program was aimed to improve the socio

---

[3] John, Karl, *Land Reform in Small Island Developing State: A Case Study on St. Vincent, West indies: 1890-2000.* (College Station, Texas, Virtualbookworm.com Publishing, 2006).

economic conditions of farmers, with a focus on "productivity" and access to credit, and began with a recognition that our land ownership patterns were a "direct heritage from colonialism".[4]

Successive governments from 1972-2000 would oversee the acquisition of all major estates for land reform purposes, including the largest being the Orange Hill Estate, acquired in 1985 and comprising 3,118 acres, acquired for the public purpose of "the provision of public housing and the improvement of agricultural production".

Post 2001, the Ralph Gonsalves Government focused on regularising title for informal settlements and continued distribution of lands. As such, 200 years after emancipation, the work to unravel the iniquities of colonialism continues.

St. Vincent and the Grenadines has not reached the stage where the acknowledgment of ancestral lands is a common narrative. There will, no doubt, come a time where the descendants of the Amerindian peoples will seek compensation for the loss of ancestral lands or at least recognition of their land rights. In the 1776 Bryers map, one can see that the northern one-third of St. Vincent was labelled as "lands granted to the Charibs by the late treaty in 1773".

---

[4] Mitchell, James, *Land Reform in the Caribbean*, (CADEC lecture at the University of the West Indies, August 29th 1972, in the collection of speeches entitled *Caribbean Crusade*, J. F. Mitchell, 1989).

The Escape Sugar Estate

The stone ruins of the Escape Estate Works were once the site of the production of sugar, rum and molasses. Nestled between these ruins are the remnants of the cast iron components of the water-powered wheel which was used to crush the sugar cane brought from the surrounding fields.

These components, as in all such works, were manufactured in Britain and brought to the island when the factory was first established in the late 18th Century.

The remains of the aqueduct are partially concealed by the vegetation above the mill. This man-made canal system supplied water from the Yambou Gorge to power the water wheels of the Escape and Argyle Sugar Mills.

Historical records show that this 193-acre estate, the property of Jonathan Morgan, Esq., was in full production by 1801. It realized peak production in 1819 with a relatively high yield per acre of 436,500 pounds (291 hogsheads) of sugar.

The cultivation of sugar cane and the production of sugar, rum and molasses were achieved at Escape using African slave labour. Approximately 195 men, women and children toiled in the fields and worked the mill, often under conditions of extreme heat and danger.

The enslaved people in the British colonies were emancipated in 1834 and the Escape Estate owner, Jonathan Morgan, was awarded compensation of £4,386 (£714,432 in today's currency[1]) for his "loss". From these proceeds, he purchased a fine Georgian townhouse at No. 8 The Circus, Bath, England. This is part of a prestigious development built from Cotswold stone and Caribbean blood.

Most of the Estates in St. Vincent continued a spiral of decline and increasing indebtedness following Emancipation.

---

[1] £4,386 in 1834 = 2024 | UK Inflation Calculator. Official Inflation Data, Alioth Finance, 22 Jan. 2024 (officialdata.org/uk/inflation/1834?amount=4386).

PART III

The Argyle Sugar Estate and East Indian Migration

The Argyle Sugar Estate existed within the boundaries of the Argyle International Airport site and was lost during its construction. However, through the collaborated effort of the SVG National Trust and the International Airport Development Company a number of pieces of machinery were salvaged and relocated.

The Argyle Sugar Mill and Estate was constructed and established in 1797 by Duncan Campbell and subsequently was inherited by the heirs of Duncan Campbell who included Prince Jules de Polignac (a French statesman, and prime minister under Charles X) and Archibald Macdonald, Esq. By 1822 there were 290 enslaved persons of African descent working on the estate.

Historical records show that in 1828 the 365-acre Argyle Sugar Estate was producing 601,500 pounds of sugar, 11,880 gallons of rum and 17,000 gallons of molasses. There were 167 enslaved persons working on the Estate at that time.

Following emancipation in 1834 the Argyle Estate owner was awarded compensation of £6,767 4s 8d (£1,102,271 in today's currency[1]) for his "loss". The former enslaved persons received no compensation for *their* hardship and immeasurable loss.

Slavery was followed by a period of apprenticeship, whereby former enslaved persons were required to work 45 hours for their former masters without compensation. This system was meant to "bridge the gap" between slavery and freedom, ensuring that the plantation economy did not face collapse. The former enslaved found it difficult to accept the continuation of compulsory labour, however, even with a new level of protection that apprenticeship afforded, including removing the power of corporal punishment from the hands of the former enslavers to the stipendiary magistrates,

---

[1] £6,767 in 1834 = £1,102,271 in 2024, UK inflation calculator. Official Inflation Data, Alioth Finance, 2nd January 2024, (officialdata.org/UK/inflation/1834?amount=67).

and the right to work elsewhere outside of the 45 hours per week. Apprentices resisted the system at the outset and asserted their rights. The freed Africans refused to work for for their former masters without pay. The system was short-lived and ended in 1838, after which many of the Africans moved off the Estate and settled in Stubbs and Victoria village. This left a shortage of labour, and the problem was addressed by the introduction of indentured labourers, first from India.

At that time, India was under British control and was facing a series of major famines. Indians wanted to escape hardship, and the British needed cheap labour for their plantations in foreign lands. Indians were considered to be meek, hardy and less rebellious, as well as adept at agriculture.[2] They were offered contracts for five-year periods to work abroad for fixed wages and a return passage home.

The first 260 Indians from southeast India (Port of Madras) arrived in St. Vincent on June 1st, 1861 (now celebrated as Indian Arrival Day), aboard the ship *Tranvancore*. Over the next two decades, a total of 2,474 Indians arrived on seven additional ships that sailed from Calcutta. The experience of the Indian indentured labourers was only marginally better than that of enslaved Africans. On October 7th, 1882 (now celebrated in St. Vincent as Indian Heritage Day), the indentured Indians marched from Argyle into Kingstown. This protest march was the beginning of the end of indentureship in St. Vincent, which occurred around 1890. St. Vincent became the first country to end Indian indentureship.

About half of the Indians who arrived in St. Vincent returned to India between 1883 and 1885.[3] Of those who stayed, many moved off the Estate and cashed in the value of their promised return passage to India, which, along with their savings, enabled them to purchase Crown lands. Approximately 1,340 remained, settling in Argyle, Calder, Akers Hill, Richland Park, Georgetown, Park Hill, Rosebank, Rosehall, and Yambou. They continued to work in farming and then moved into trade and light manufacturing.

---

[2] Thomas, Lenroy. *Stories from Our Indian Elders* (self-published, 2021).
[3] Thomas, Arnold. *The Argyle Chronicles* (Presentation made at UWI Centre for Continuing Studies, 30 May, 2006).

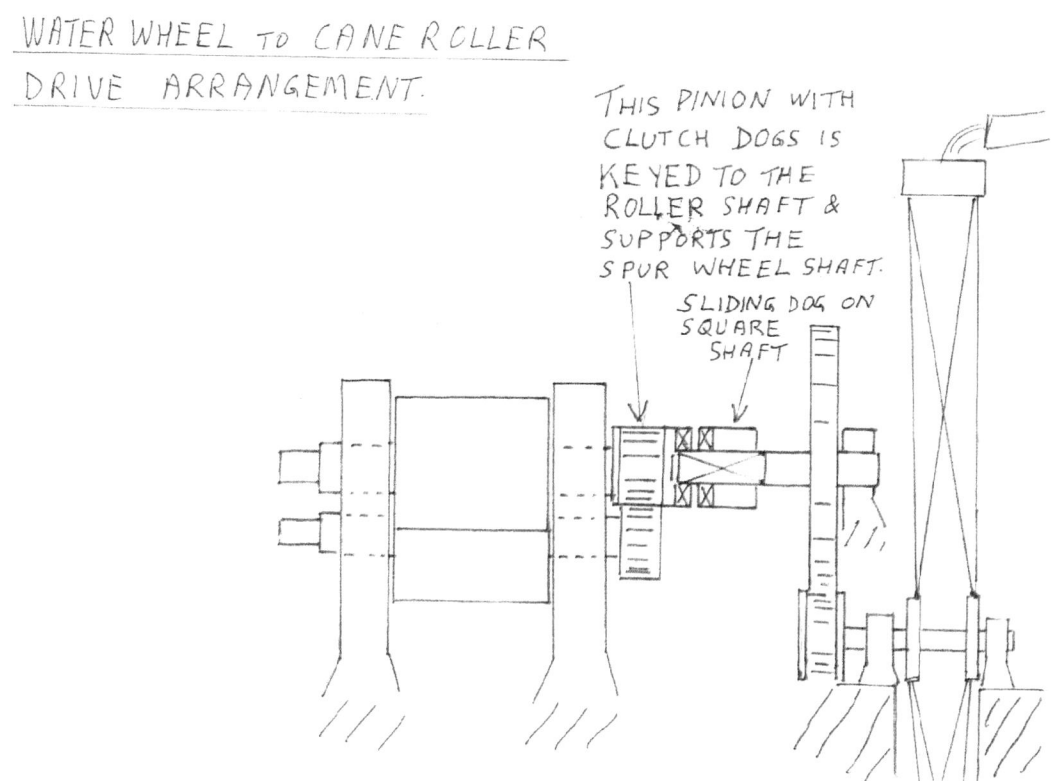

Engineering at Argyle Sugar Mill.
Wheel on right, crusher on left.
Drawing by engineers at the University of Hartford

CONCLUSION

Across the world, rock art in the form of paintings and engravings is a lasting artistic expression of the belief systems and thoughts of our ancestors, of which many sites are recognized by UNESCO. The rock art of St. Vincent and the Grenadines has been short-listed with UNESCO as a world heritage site, due to the exceptional universal value it holds as evidence of the great migration of humankind across the globe. The similarity in the images of rock art found in St. Vincent with that of rock art throughout the Lesser and Greater Antilles, as well as that of the mainland of South America, demonstrates the historic ties that bind the islands with the cultures of the Orinoco river. Our ancestors navigated the Caribbean Sea in dug-out canoes, carved by hand from ancient trees and propelled by human strength. They transcended the boundaries of nation states, with a freedom of movement that eludes us today. Every petroglyph site in St. Vincent created on basalt rock, stands strategically near a body of water, be it a river or the sea, demonstrating the strong connection of our ancestors with their environment. Indeed the lie of the land, the streams, the foliage and the cosmos encompassing the petroglyph sites are integral to and indivisible from the sacred petroglyph art form.

The messages in the rocks left to us by our ancestors, seen in the petroglyphs at Argyle and throughout St. Vincent and the Grenadines, is a type of historic writing that is not tarnished by biases or prejudices. It tells a face value story of cultural life in pre-Columbian times that needs to be preserved for all future generations. All petroglyphs of St. Vincent,

Martins' Petroglyph Park

Sandy Bay Work Stones

be they the engravings of Yambou I (Argyle), the multiple carvings by the Yambou river in the Mesopotamia Valley (Yambou II -VII), the cup holes known as the '13 stones' at Chateaubelair, the Buccament rock shelter petroglyphs or the work stones at Spring Bay, Bequia, should be declared by the Government, through the National Trust, as protected national heritage sites and preserved in situ in their majestic surroundings for all future generations of Vincentians.

The Martins' Petroglyph Park (photo below), where the Yambou I and Yambou VIII petroglyphs were relocated, and whose development was initiated by the National Trust with the support from the Canadian Fund for Local Initiatives, should be given further support as a field park dedicated to telling the story of the history of Argyle from indigenous times, through to colonialism and enslavement, to the time of the arrival of East Indians aboard the *Travancore* and beyond. It should celebrate the resistance of our native peoples to oppression and colonialism. Along with Dominica, we were the last islands to hold out against the crushing power of the Europeans.

This booklet has touched on the history of enslavement and indentureship centred around the 19th century colonial plantations at Argyle and Escape. The magnitude of the sugar exports generated from Argyle and Escape alone, demonstrate how much of our African and Indian ancestors' blood and sweat was sacrificed in the building of the riches of the British Empire.

As a young nation, as we navigate our place in the world, we must first acknowledge and understand the roads travelled by our ancestors and give them a place of honour in our national historical narrative.

Acknowledgements

I wish to thank the contributors to this book: Kathy Martin, Deirdre Millington-Myers, Nicola Redway and Dr. Adrian Fraser.

I also wish to thank Chairperson of the National Trust Descima Alexander-Hamilton for her friendship, support and commitment to heritage conservation.

I am grateful to Kathy Martin, a Vincentian National Treasure. She has and continues to work tirelessly for the preservation of our national patrimony. She is a true unsung hero. She has been my greatest inspiration in documenting our heritage. She took me to the fields of Argyle and introduced me to the experience of touching an artifact that had been buried for hundreds of years.

I am grateful to the Manager of the National Trust Laverne Bentick-Phillips, the wheel of the Trust.

I value greatly Osei Morris, Trustee, for his support and dedication to heritage conservation.

I wish to thank Morrison Baisden for inspiring me to tell a revisionist story where it is needed.

I also wish to thank Dr. Arnold Thomas and Junior Bacchus for documenting and sharing with me our Indian history.

I remember fondly two patrons of the National Trust, Christian I. Martin, CMG and His Excellency Sir Frederick Ballantyne, of blessed memory, for the confidence they placed in me, and for their contribution to the longevity of the SVG National Trust.

I wish to thank Marc Erdrich and Ruth Boerger; they made putting this booklet together an enjoyable journey.

I wish to thank Patricia Mitchell and Sir James Mitchell for encouraging me to write.

www.ingramcontent.com/pod-product-compliance
Lightning Source LLC
LaVergne TN
LVRC080725070526
838199LV00042B/741